DRAGO

STONEHENGE SUNSET

The sun's eye prises
splinters of granite
drawn like dragonsteeth
in the earth's bunched shrug :

watches stones stiffen
into sinews as men
appear, thighs taut for
sacrifice. The eye

is speared open. A
smear of blood waits for
night to wipe clear the
memory of pain.

And then, if day is
granted them, these men
will stride to freedom,
arms stretched in greeting.

Eric Williams

DRAGONSTEETH

edited by Eric Williams

EDWARD ARNOLD

© Eric Williams 1972

First published 1972
by Edward Arnold (Publishers) Ltd,
25 Hill Street
London W1X 8LL

Reprinted 1972, 1973

Reprinted 1974 for Edward Arnold Australia
373 Bay Street
Port Melbourne
Victoria 3207
Australia

ISBN: 0 7267 0009 6

Printed in Great Britain by
Fletcher & Son Ltd, Norwich

Preface

This anthology is designed for pupils aged 13–15 (although much of its material could be enjoyed by groups above or below this age range) and has been used, both as successful reading material and to kindle vigorous discussion and sensitive writing, in English lessons with classes of varying ages and abilities. But the success of this collection has also been in encouraging adolescents (some of them wary or even hostile in their previous attitude) to regard reading poetry as a challenging, often disturbing, but always enjoyable experience: and it is greatly aided in this by the addition of the many photographs that make this volume attractive and exciting to use.

But the purpose of the photographs is not merely decorative for they make their own positive contribution, throwing the poetry into sharp relief, widening its implications and underlining its themes, and they will prove equally useful as starting points for creative work in the classroom.

The poems, together with the photographs, explore man's physical setting—the seasons, weather, elements, sea, landscape, etc.—and the crises and emotions they arouse in him; and particularly man's relation with the other animals that surround him, both literally and in the imagery through which they haunt his writing. But there is no arbitrary division of the material into themes, for it would be impossible (and highly undesirable) to classify these poems into abstractions: each deals with a specific, vital, direct experience whose relevance will strike the pupil immediately, with no need of any explanatory labels. And I have been particularly concerned to make the anthology intelligible as a unity. Each poem has been placed with great care in the position in which it will make its most effective impact when read in relation to those that surround it. None exists in isolation: the poems work collectively in the same way as the pictures do, enlarging and commenting on the situations and issues they present. A few established favourites are included here, as well as some not so familiar: an effect of this anthology's presentation is that poems already heavily 'anthologised' can be seen in a fresh light because of the other poems and pictures that surround them. The format of this book has similarly been designed so that this relationship is immediately visible when the 'double spread' lies open on the pupil's desk.

Thus the poems can be read either singly or together. As there is, broadly speaking, a circular movement to the anthology following the progress of the seasons and returning to its starting point, teachers will find it easy to detach a segment for use in conjunction with their work in progress.

E.W.

CONTENTS

You'd Better Believe Him	Brian Patten	9
Mountain Lion	D. H. Lawrence	10
Hard Frost	Andrew Young	11
The Boy Fishing	E. J. Scovell	11
Feeding Ducks	Norman MacCaig	12
Dawn Shoot	Seamus Heaney	12
First Blood	Jon Stallworthy	13
The Gallows	Edward Thomas	14
The Wasps' Nest	George Macbeth	15
Starlings	David Sutton	15
The Horses	Ted Hughes	15
The Beasts	Walt Whitman	17
Trout	Seamus Heaney	17
Pike	Ted Hughes	18
Polecats in Breconshire	Ted Walker	22
The Frog	Anon	22
Hedgehog	Miles Gibson	22
Considering the Snail	Thom Gunn	23
Riddle	Kevin Crossley-Holland	23
Mallard	Rex Warner	24
Bats	George Macbeth	26
The Fox	C. Day Lewis	27
Two Performing Elephants	D. H. Lawrence	27
Their Lonely Betters	W. H. Auden	27
Together	Siegfried Sassoon	28
The Runaway	Robert Frost	28
A Small Dragon	Brian Patten	28
Caught by Chance	T. W. Ramsey	29
The Caged Bird in Springtime	James Kirkup	30
Caring for Animals	Jon Silkin	30
'Shape Poem'	Stefan Themerson	31
Cat	Michael Hamburger	32
The Cat	Edward Brathwaite	32
Esther's Tomcat	Ted Hughes	33
Fog	Carl Sandburg	34
The Fog	F. R. McCreary	34
The Ship	Richard Church	35
Wind	Ted Hughes	36
House for Sale	Vernon Scannell	37
A Windy Day	Andrew Young	37
The House Martins	Michael Hamburger	38
Riddle	Kevin Crossley-Holland	38
The Postman	Jon Stallworthy	38
A Removal from Terry Street	Douglas Dunn	39
Riddle	Kevin Crossley-Holland	39
Thrushes	Humbert Wolfe	39
Thaw on a Building Site	Norman MacCaig	40
The Builders	Hugo Williams	41
Cranes	J. R. S. Davies	41
April Day: Binsey	Michael Hamburger	42
April Rise	Laurie Lee	42
Girl, Boy, Flower, Bicycle	M. K. Joseph	42
A Negro Woman	William Carlos Williams	44

On Roofs of Terry Street	Douglas Dunn	44
Day of These Days	Laurie Lee	45
Summer Farm	Norman MacCaig	46
Pigeons	Richard Kell	47
Apples	Laurie Lee	50
Unharvested	Robert Frost	50
Windfalls	Ian Hamilton	50
Blackberry-Picking	Seamus Heaney	51
Evening After Rain	David Sutton	51
Quiet	Richard Church	52
Hedgehog	Anthony Thwaite	52
The Listeners	Walter de la Mare	52
Late Night Walk Down Terry Street	Douglas Dunn	55
The 'Alice Jean'	Robert Graves	56
John Polruddon	Charles Causley	57
From the Night-Window	Douglas Dunn	58
The Projectionist's Nightmare	Brian Patten	59
Interruption to a Journey	Norman MacCaig	60
Ambulance	Miles Gibson	60
The Casualty	Ted Hughes	60
Survivors	Alan Ross	62
The Rescue	Ted Hughes	62
Psalm of Those Who Go Forth Before Daylight	Carl Sandburg	64
Father's Gloves	Ted Walker	64
Soil	R. S. Thomas	65
Kite	Miles Gibson	66
Gale Warning	Michael Roberts	66
Thistles	Ted Hughes	68
Mushrooms	Sylvia Plath	68
Dream	Seamus Heaney	69
The Harvest Field	W. R. Rodgers	70
Men In Green	David Campbell	70
View of a Pig	Ted Hughes	71
The Last Whale	Miles Gibson	72
A Dead Mole	Andrew Young	72
Little Fable	Roy Fuller	72
Field of Autumn	Laurie Lee	73
Game's End	David Sutton	74
Throwing a Tree : New Forest	Thomas Hardy	75
Coal Fire	Louis Untermeyer	79
For Bonfires	Edwin Morgan	79
Robin	Hal Summers	83
Winter the Huntsman	Osbert Sitwell	84
The Winter Trees	Clifford Dyment	85
The Computer's First Christmas Card	Edwin Morgan	86
Chartres Windows : Winter	Paula Claire	87
Sleet	Norman MacCaig	88
Home	Ian Hamilton	88
Sunday Afternoons	Anthony Thwaite	88
The Battle	Louis Simpson	90
Owls	Glyn Hughes	91
The Thought-Fox	Ted Hughes	91

YOU'D BETTER BELIEVE HIM
A Fable

Discovered an old rocking-horse in Woolworth's,
He tried to feed it but without much luck
So he stroked it, had a long conversation about
The trees it came from, the attics it had visited.
Tried to take it out then
But the store detective he
Called the police who in court next morning said
'He acted strangely when arrested,
His statement read simply ''I believe in rocking-
horses.''
We have reason to believe him mad.'
'Quite so,' said the prosecution,
'Bring in the rocking-horse as evidence.'
'I'm afraid it's escaped, sir,' said the store manager,
'Left a hoof print as evidence
On the skull of the store detective.'
'Quite so,' said the prosecution, fearful
of the neighing
Out in the corridor.

Brian Patten

MOUNTAIN LION

Climbing through the January snow, into the Lobo canyon
Dark grow the spruce-trees, blue is the balsam, water sounds still unfrozen, and the trail is still evident.

Men!
Two men!
Men! The only animal in the world to fear!

Then we all advance, to meet

Two Mexicans, strangers, emerging out of the dark and snow and inwardness of the Lobo valley.
What are you doing here on this vanishing trail?

What is he carrying?
Something yellow.
A deer?

Que tiene, amigo?
Leon—

He smiles, foolishly, as if he were caught doing wrong.
And we smile, foolishly, as if we didn't know.
He is quite gentle and dark-faced.

It is a mountain lion,
A long, long slim cat, yellow like a lioness.
Dead.
He trapped her this morning, he says, smiling foolishly.

Lift up her face,
Her round, bright face, bright as frost.
Her round, fine-fashioned head, with two dead ears;
And stripes in the brilliant frost of her face, sharp, fine, dark rays,

Dark, keen, fine eyes in the brilliant frost of her face.
Beautiful dead eyes.

Hermoso es!

They go out towards the open;
We go on into the gloom of Lobo.
And above the trees I found her lair,
A hole in the blood-orange brilliant rocks that stick up, a little cave.
And bones, and twigs, and a perilous ascent.

So, she will never leap up that way again, with the yellow flash of a mountain lion's long shoot!
And her bright striped frost-face will never watch any more, out of the shadow of the cave in the blood-orange rock,
Above the trees of the Lobo dark valley-mouth!

Instead, I look out.
And out to the rim of the desert, like a dream, never real;
To the snow of the Sangre de Cristo mountains, the ice of the mountains of Picoris.
And near across at the opposite steep of snow, green trees motionless standing in snow, like a Christmas toy.
And I think in this empty world there was room for me and a mountain lion.
And I think in the world beyond, how easily we might spare a million or two of humans
And never miss them.
Yet what a gap in the world, the missing white frost-face of that slim yellow mountain lion!

D. H. Lawrence

HARD FROST

Frost called to water 'Halt!'
And crusted the moist snow with sparkling salt;
Brooks, their own bridges, stop,
And icicles in long stalactites drop,
And tench in water-holes
Lurk under gluey glass like fish in bowls.

In the hard-rutted lane
At every footstep breaks a brittle pane,
And twinkling trees ice-bound
Changed into weeping willows, sweep the ground;
Dead boughs take roots in ponds
And ferns on windows shoot their ghostly fronds.

But vainly the fierce frost
Interns poor fish, ranks trees in an armed host,
Hangs daggers from house-eaves
And on the windows ferny ambush weaves;
In the long war grown warmer
The sun will strike him dead and strip his armour.

Andrew Young

THE BOY FISHING

I am cold and alone,
On my tree-root sitting as cold as stone.
The fish come to my net. I scorned the sun,
The voices on the road, and they have gone.
My eyes are buried in the cold pond, under
The cold, spread leaves, my thoughts are silver-wet.
I have ten stickleback, a half-day's plunder,
Safe in my jar. I shall have ten more yet.

E. J. Scovell

FEEDING DUCKS

One duck stood on my toes.
The others made watery rushes after bread
Thrown by my momentary hand; instead
She stood duck-still and got far more than those.

An invisible drone boomed by
With a beetle in it; the neighbour's yearning bull
Bugled across five fields. And an evening full
Of other evenings quietly began to die.

And my everlasting hand
Dropped on my hypocrite duck her grace of bread.
And I thought, 'The first to be fattened, the first to
be dead',
Till my gestures enlarged, wide over the darkening
land.

Norman MacCaig

DAWN SHOOT

Clouds ran their wet mortar, plastered the daybreak
Grey. The stones clicked tartly
If we missed the sleepers but mostly
Silent we headed up the railway
Where now the only stream was funnelling from
cows
Ditched on their rumps beyond hedges,
Cudding, watching, and knowing.
The rails scored a bull's-eye into the eye
Of a bridge. A corncrake challenged
Unexpectedly like a hoarse sentry
And a snipe rocketed away on reconnaissance.

Rubber-booted, belted, tense as two parachutists,
We climbed the iron gate and dropped
Into the meadow's six acres of broom, gorse and
dew.

A sandy bank, reinforced with coiling roots,
Faced you, two hundred yards from the track.
Snug on our bellies behind a rise of dead whins,
Our ravenous eyes getting used to the greyness,
We settled, soon had the holes under cover.
This was the den they all would be heading for now,
Loping under ferns in dry drains, flashing
Brown orbits across ploughlands and grazing.

The plaster thinned at the skyline, the whitewash
Was bleaching on houses and stables,
The cock would be sounding reveille
In seconds.
And there was one breaking
In from the gap in the corner.

Donnelly's left hand came up
And came down on my barrel. This one was his.
'For Christ's sake,' I spat, 'Take your time, there'll
be more'
There was the playboy trotting up to the hole
By the ash tree, 'Wild rover no more',
Said Donnelly and emptied two barrels
And got him. I finished him off.

Another snipe catapulted into the light,
A mare whinnied and shivered her haunches
Up on a hill. The others would not be back
After three shots like that. We dandered off
To the railway; the prices were small at that time
So we did not bother to cut out the tongue.
The ones that slipped back when the all clear got
round
Would be first to examine him.

Seamus Heaney

FIRST BLOOD

It was. The breech smelling of oil,
The stock of resin—buried snug
In the shoulder. Not too much recoil
At the firing of the first slug

(Jubilantly into the air)
Not yet too little. Targets pinned
Against a tree : shot down : and there
Abandoned to the sniping wind.

My turn first to carry the gun.
Indian file and camouflaged
With contours of green shade and sun
We ghosted between larch and larch.

A movement between branches—thump
Of a fallen cone. The barrel
Jumps, making branches jump
Higher, dislodging the squirrel

To the next tree. Your turn, my turn.
The silhouette retracts its head.
A hit. 'Let's go back to the lawn.'
'We can't leave it carrying lead

'For the rest of its life. Reload.
Finish him off. Reload again.'
It was now *him*, and when he showed
The sky cracked like a window pane.

He broke away : traversed a full
Half dozen trees : vanished. Had found
A hole ? We watched that terrible
Slow spiral to the clubbing ground.

His back was to the tree. His eyes
Were gun barrels. He was dumb,
And we could not see past the size
Of his hands or hear for the drum

In his side. Four shots point-blank
To dull his eyes, a fifth to stop
The shiver in his clotted flank.
A fling of earth. As we stood up

The larches closed their ranks. And when
Earth would not muffle the drumming blood
We, like dishonoured soldiers, ran
The gauntlet of a darkening wood.

Jon Stallworthy

THE GALLOWS

There was a weasel lived in the sun
With all his family,
Till a keeper shot him with his gun
And hung him up on a tree,
Where he swings in the wind and rain,
In the sun and in the snow,
Without pleasure, without pain,
On the dead oak tree bough.

There was a crow who was no sleeper,
But a thief and a murderer
Till a very late hour ; and this keeper
Made him one of the things that were,
To hang and flap in rain and wind,
In the sun and in the snow,
There are no more sins to be sinned
On the dead oak tree bough.

There was a magpie, too,
Had a long tongue and a long tail ;
He could both talk and do—
But what did that avail ?
He, too, flaps in the wind and rain
Alongside weasel and crow,
Without pleasure, without pain,
On the dead oak tree bough.

And many other beasts
And birds, skin, bone, and feather,
Have been taken from their feasts
And hung up there together,
To swing and have endless leisure
In the sun and in the snow,
Without pain, without pleasure,
On the dead oak tree bough.

Edward Thomas

THE WASPS' NEST

All day to the loose tile behind the parapet
The droning bombers fled : in the wet gutter
Belly-upwards the dead were lying, numbed
By October cold. And now the bloat queen,
Sick-orange, with wings draped, and feelers
trailing,
Like Helen combing her hair, posed on the ledge
Twenty feet above the traffic. I watched, just a foot
From her eyes, very glad of the hard glass parting
My pressed human nose from her angry sting
And her heavy power to warn the cold future
Sunk in unfertilised eggs. And I thought : if I reached
And inched this window open, and cut her in half
With my unclasped penknife, I could exterminate
An unborn generation. All next summer,
If she survives, the stepped roof will swarm
With a jam of striped fighters. Therefore, this winter
In burning sulphur in their dug-out hangars
All the bred wasps must die. Unless I kill her.
So I balanced assassination with genocide
As the queen walked on the ledge, a foot from my
eyes
In the last sun of the year, the responsible man
With a cold nose, who knew that he must kill,
Coming to no sure conclusion, nor anxious to come.

George Macbeth

STARLINGS

My father got up determinedly that Sunday.
'Those starlings had their boots on again last night.
I'll have to clear them out, before they lay.'
I did not approve. But then I did not sleep in the room
On top of which they kept such a brawling
And such a loving, in the dawn's small hours.

He poked a ladder up through the loft and climbed,
Descending some time later with a pailful
Of straw and mud, mixed with a few soft feathers.
('Breast feathers', I said), the remnants of four nests,
And threw them in the hedge. And I suppose
He could not do much else ; but later on
You should have heard the clamour as those starlings
Came crying desolate about the eaves,
Stirring us each with some uneasiness,
Their wings above the windows beating at
The closed doors of our pity or our guilt,
Like old wrongdoings coming home to roost.

David Sutton

THE HORSES

I climbed through woods in the hour-before-dawn
dark.
Evil air, a frost-making stillness,

Not a leaf, not a bird,—
A world cast in frost. I came out above the wood

Where my breath left tortuous statues in the iron
light.
But the valleys were draining the darkness

Till the moorline—blackening dregs of the
brightening grey—
Halved the sky ahead. And I saw the horses :

Huge in the dense grey—ten together—
Megalith-still. They breathed, making no move,

With draped manes and tilted hind-hooves,
Making no sound.

I passed : not one snorted or jerked its head.
Grey silent fragments

Of a grey silent world.

I listened in emptiness on the moor-ridge.
The curlew's tear turned its edge on the silence.

Slowly detail leafed from the darkness. Then the sun
Orange, red, red erupted

Silently, and splitting to its core tore and flung cloud,
Shook the gulf open, showed blue,

And the big planets hanging—
I turned

Stumbling in the fever of a dream, down towards
The dark woods, from the kindling tops,

And came to the horses.
　　　　　　　　There, still they stood,
But now streaming and glistening under the flow of
light,

Their draped stone manes, their tilted hind-hooves
Stirring under a thaw while all around them

The frost showed its fires. But still they made no
sound.
Not one snorted or stamped,

Their hung heads patient as the horizons,
High over valleys, in the red levelling rays—

In din of the crowded streets, going among the
years, the faces,
May I still meet my memory in so lonely a place

Between the streams and the red clouds, hearing
curlews,
Hearing the horizons endure.

Ted Hughes

THE BEASTS

I think I could turn and live with animals, they are so placid and self-contained
I stand and look at them long and long.
They do not sweat and whine about their condition;
They do not lie awake in the dark and weep for their sins;
They do not make me sick discussing their duty to God;
Not one is dissatisfied—not one is demented with the mania of owning things;
Not one kneels to another, nor to his kind that lived thousands of years ago;
Not one is respectable and industrious over the whole earth.

Walt Whitman

TROUT

Hangs, a fat gun-barrel,
deep under arched bridges
or slips like butter down
the throat of the river.

From depths smooth-skinned as plums
his muzzle gets bull's eye;
picks off grass-seed and moths
that vanish, torpedoed.

Where water unravels
over gravel-beds he
is fired from the shallows
white belly reporting

flat; darts like a tracer-
bullet back between stones
and is never burnt out.
A volley of cold blood

ramrodding the current.

Seamus Heaney

PIKE

Pike, three inches long, perfect
Pike in all parts, green tigering the gold.
Killers from the egg : the malevolent aged grin.
They dance on the surface among the flies.

Or move, stunned by their own grandeur,
Over a bed of emerald, silhouette
Of submarine delicacy and horror.
A hundred feet long in their world.

In ponds, under the heat-struck lily pads—
Gloom of their stillness :
Logged on last year's black leaves, watching
upwards.
Or hung in an amber cavern of weeds.

The jaws' hooked clamp and fangs
Not to be changed at this date ;
A life subdued to its instrument ;
The gills kneading quietly, and the pectorals.

Three we kept behind glass,
Jungled in weed : three inches, four,
And four and a half : fed fry to them—
Suddenly there were two. Finally one

With a sag belly and the grin it was born with.
And indeed they spare nobody.
Two, six pounds each, over two feet long,
High and dry and dead in the willow-herb—

One jammed past its gills down the other's gullet :
The outside eye stared : as a vice locks—
The same iron in this eye
Though its film shrank in death.

A pond I fished, fifty yards across,
Whose lilies and muscular tench
Had outlasted every visible stone
Of the monastery that planted them—

Stilled legendary depth :
It was as deep as England. It held
Pike too immense to stir, so immense and old
That past nightfall I dared not cast

But silently cast and fished
With the hair frozen on my head
For what might move, for what eye might move.
The still splashes on the dark pond,

Owls hushing the floating woods
Frail on my ear against the dream
Darkness beneath night's darkness had freed,
That rose slowly towards me, watching.

Ted Hughes

POLECATS IN BRECONSHIRE

Fine moths dropped from the darkness,
drifted like fallings of swarf
to dust the grasses whitely
where whitely flew the first scarf
of an owl as quiet as wool.

It was time for them to come
hot from a clammy chamber
under the summer mountain,
test the close air, and clamber
the foul chippings at their door.

They stood, rare as royalty,
in black and purplish fur
matted with the sweat of sleep;
relaxed as flaccid rubber,
they were ready to be stretched

the length of night's territory.
Seldom glimpsed by a human—
except, perhaps, at evening
by lonely widow-women
musty as old whinberries—

they loped for no enemy
they knew. Over the bracken
they leaped free; among the few
too few to count, five of them ran,
their bodies smooth in the dew.

And all the while there was night
they would shark through the thickets,
incising behind the skull
beasts that would be the pellets
of their pleasure. Armoured with

stench, and teeth to score tungsten,
they would slummock on fat eels.

On some road the good mother
would suckle her whelps. I would wonder
what they were, under my wheels.

Ted Walker

THE FROG

What a wonderful bird the frog are—
When he stand he sit almost;
When he hops, he flies almost.
He ain't got no sense hardly:
He ain't got no tail hardly either.
When he sit, he sit on what he ain't got almost.

Anon

HEDGEHOG

no one
remembers it
crossing the road

it was—simply—there

armed to the teeth
ugly with fleas
it grunted
in the morning light

and curled up
like a mine

just waiting

for someone
to step out of line

Miles Gibson

CONSIDERING THE SNAIL

The snail pushes through a green
night, for the grass is heavy
with water and meets over
the bright path he makes, where rain
has darkened the earth's dark. He
moves in a wood of desire,

pale antlers barely stirring
as he hunts. I cannot tell
what power is at work, drenched there
with purpose, knowing nothing.
What is a snail's fury ? All
I think is that if later

I parted the blades above
the tunnel and saw the thin
trail of broken white across
litter, I would never have
imagined the slow passion
to that deliberate progress.

Thom Gunn

RIDDLE

Silent is my dress when I step across the earth,
Reside in my house, or ruffle the waters.
Sometimes my adornments and this high windy air
Lift me over the livings of men,
The power of the clouds carries me far
Over all people. My white pinions
Resound very loudly, ring with a melody,
Sing out clearly, when I sleep not on
The soil or settle on grey waters . . . a travelling
spirit.

(*Answer p. 96*) *translated from the Old English
by Kevin Crossley-Holland*

MALLARD

Squawking they rise from reeds into the sun,
climbing like furies, running on blood and bone,
with wings like garden-shears clipping the misty air,
four mallard, hard-winged, with necks like rods
fly in perfect formation over the marsh.

Keeping their distance, gyring, not letting slip the air,
but leaping into it straight like hounds or divers,
they stretch out into the wind and sound their horns
again.

Suddenly siding to a bank of air unbidden
by hand signal or morse message of command
downsky they plane, sliding like corks on a current,
designed so deftly that all air is advantage,

till with few flaps, orderly as they left earth,
alighting among curlew they pad on mud.

Rex Warner

BATS

have no accidents. They loop
their incredible horse-shoe
loops, dead-stop

on air-brakes,
road-safe on
squeaks : racketeering

their SOS noise in a
jai-alai
bat-jam

of collapsed umbrellas, a
Chancery Lane
of avoided

collisions, all in a
cave without lights : then
hung

happy, a snore
of strap-hangers
undergrounding

without an *Evening
Standard* between them
to the common Waterloo

that awaits bats, like
all beasts, then
off now, zoom !

Man, you can't even
hear them ; bats,
are they ?

George Macbeth

THE FOX

'Look, it's a fox !'—their two hearts spoke
Together. A fortunate day
That was when they saw him, a russet spark
Blown from the wood's long-smouldering dark
On to the woodside quay.

There, on the ride, a dog fox paused.
Around him the shadows lay
Attentive suddenly, masked and poised ;
And the watchers found themselves enclosed
In a circuit stronger than they.

He stood for some mystery only shared
By creatures of fire and clay.
They watched him stand with the masterless air
Of one who had the best right to be there—
Let other go or stay ;

Then, with a flick of his long brush, sign
The moment and whisk it away.
Time flowed back, and the two walked on
Down the valley. They felt they were given a sign—
But of what, they could hardly say.

C. Day Lewis

TWO PERFORMING ELEPHANTS

He stands with his forefeet on the drum
and the other, the old one, the pallid hoary female
must creep her great bulk beneath the bridge of him.

On her knees, in utmost caution
all agog, and curling up her trunk
she edges through without upsetting him.
Triumph ! the ancient, pig-tailed monster !

When her trick is to climb over him
with what shadow-like slow carefulness
she skims him, sensitive
as shadows from the ages gone and perished
in touching him, and planting her round feet.

While the wispy, modern children, half-afraid
watch silent. The looming of the hoary, far-gone ages
is too much for them.

D. H. Lawrence

THEIR LONELY BETTERS

As I listened from a beach-chair in the shade
To all the noises that my garden made,
It seemed to me only proper that words
Should be witheld from vegetables and birds.

A robin with no Christian name ran through
The Robin-Anthem which was all it knew,
And rustling flowers for some third party waited
To say which pairs, if any, should get mated.

Not one of them was capable of lying,
There was not one which knew that it was dying
Or could have with a rhythm or a rhyme
Assumed responsibility for time.

Let them leave language to their lonely betters
Who count some days and long for certain letters ;
We, too, make noises when we laugh or weep,
Words are for those with promises to keep.

W. H. Auden

TOGETHER

Splashing along the boggy woods all day,
And over brambled hedge and holding clay,
I shall not think of him:
But when the watery fields grow brown and dim,
And hounds have lost their fox, and horses tire,
I know that he'll be with me on my way
Home through the darkness to the evening fire.

He's jumped each stile along the glistening lanes;
His hand will be upon the mud-soaked reins;
Hearing the saddle creak,
He'll wonder if the frost will come next week.
I shall forget him in the morning light;
And while we gallop on he will not speak:
But at the stable-door he'll say good-night.

Siegfried Sassoon

THE RUNAWAY

Once when the snow of the year was beginning to fall,
We stopped by a mountain pasture to say, 'Whose colt?'
A little Morgan had one forefoot on the wall,
The other curled at his breast. He dipped his head
And snorted at us. And then he had to bolt.
We heard the miniature thunder where he fled,
And we saw him, or thought we saw him, dim and grey,
Like a shadow against the curtain of falling flakes.
'I think the little fellow's afraid of the snow.
He isn't winter-broken. It isn't play
With the little fellow at all. He's running away.

I doubt if even his mother could tell him, "Sakes,
It's only weather." He'd think she didn't know!
Where is his mother? He can't be out alone.'
And now he comes again with a clatter of stone,
And mounts the wall again with whited eyes
And all his tail that isn't hair up straight.
He shudders his coat as if to throw off flies.
'Whoever it is that leaves him out so late,
When other creatures have gone to stall and bin,
Ought to be told to come and take him in.'

Robert Frost

A SMALL DRAGON

I've found a small dragon in the woodshed.
Think it must have come from deep inside a forest
because it's damp and green and leaves
are still reflecting in its eyes.

I fed it on many things, tried grass,
the roots of stars, hazel-nut and dandelion,
but it stared up at me as if to say, I need
foods you can't provide.

It made a nest among the coal,
not unlike a bird's but larger,
it is out of place here
and is quite silent.

If you believed in it I would come
hurrying to your house to let you share my wonder,
but I want instead to see
if you yourself will pass this way.

Brian Patten

CAUGHT BY CHANCE

I found you fluttering,
Caught in a net
Wild with terror,
With the dew wet.

With care and toil
I cut you free,
Hope balanced fear
As you looked at me.

The meshes had scraped
A wing-blade raw,
You held my finger
In one clenched claw,

While I cut and cut
The meshes away;
And trembling
In my hand you lay

While I watched your quivering
Breast with sorrow—
Doubting if you
Would see the morrow;

Seeing a pattern
In your distress
Of our despair
And helplessness.

Still next morning
Wet with rain,
Rigid I found you
—All in vain

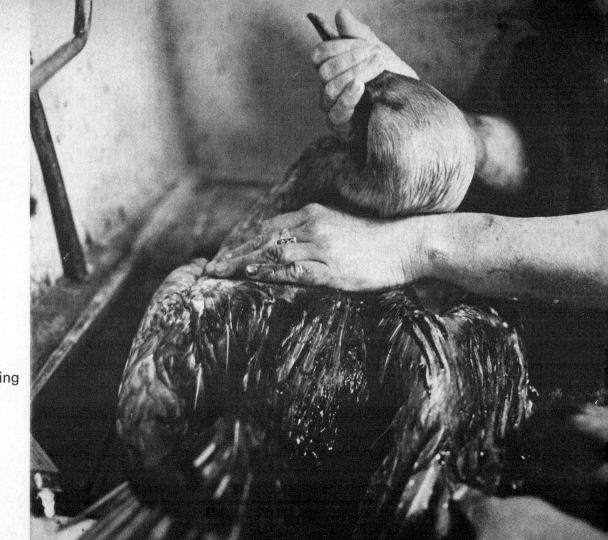

The care and toil
Empty the hope,
So little it lies
In human scope

To help the feeble
As weak as they,
And only living
From day to day.

Cold as the earth
The cold rain beat
I found you, and with you
My own defeat.

T. W. Ramsey

CARING FOR ANIMALS

I ask sometimes why these small animals
With bitter eyes, why we should care for them.

I question the sky, the serene blue water,
But it cannot say. It gives no answer.

And no answer releases in my head
A procession of grey shades patched and
whimpering :

THE CAGED BIRD IN SPRINGTIME

What can it be,
This curious anxiety ?
It is as if I wanted
To fly away from here.

But how absurd !
I have never flown in my life,
And I do not know
What flying means, though I have heard,
Of course, something about it.

Why do I peck the wires of this little cage ?
It is the only nest I have ever known.
But I want to build my own,
High in the secret branches of the air.

I cannot quite remember how
It is done, but I know
That what I want to do
Cannot be done here.

I have all I need—
Seed and water, air and light.
Why, then, do I weep with anguish,
And beat my head and my wings
Against those sharp wires, while the children
Smile at each other, saying : 'Hark how he sings' ?

James Kirkup

Dogs with clipped ears, wheezing cart horses
A fly without shadow and without thought.

Is it with these menaces to our vision
With this procession led by a man carrying wood

We must be concerned ? The holy land, the rearing
Green island should be kindlier than this.

Yet the animals, our ghosts, need tending to.
Take in the whipped cat and the blinded owl ;

Take up the man-trapped squirrel upon your shoulder.
Attend to the unnecessary beasts.

From growing mercy and a moderate love
Great love for the human animal occurs.

And your love grows. Your great love grows and grows.

Jon Silkin

Heigh
my large   flowing mane
three powerful   coarse   and
solid-hoofed   long   tail
domesticated mammals with

all   all   all
your   your   your
3 × 4   3 × 4   3 × 4
feet   feet   feet
in   in   having
the   the   no
air   invisible   foundation in any substance
together   elastic   capable
            gaseous substance   of
            which   resisting
            surrounds   penetration
            the Earth   by other
                                    substances

at one stage of each stride ;

Stefan Themerson

CAT

Unfussy lodger, she knows what she wants and gets
it :
Food, cushions, fires, the run of the garden.
I, her night porter in the small hours
Don't bother to grumble, grimly let her in.
To that coldness she purrs assent,
Eats her fill and outwits me,
Plays hide and seek in the dark house.

Only at times, by chance meeting the gaze
Of her amber eyes that can rest on me
As on a beech-bole, on bracken or meadow grass
I'm moved to celebrate the years between us,
The farness and the nearness :
My fingers graze her head.
To that fondness she purrs assent.

Michael Hamburger

THE CAT

To plan plan to create to have
Whiskers cool carat silver ready and curved
Bristling

To plan plan to create to have
Eyes green doors that dilate greenest
Pouncers

To be ready rubber ball ready
Feet bouncers cool fluid in
Tension

To be steady steady claws all
Attention to wait wait and create
Pouncing

To be a cat eeling through alleys
Slipping through windows of odours
To feel swiftness slowly

To halt halt at the gate hearing
Unlocking whispers paper feet wrapping
Potatoes and papers

To hear nicely mice spider feet
Scratching greatly horny nails
Catching a fire flies wire legs stretch stretch-

Ing beyond this arch
Untriumphant lazily rubb-
Ing the soft fur of home

Edward Brathwaite

ESTHER'S TOMCAT

Daylong this tomcat lies stretched flat
As an old rough mat, no mouth and no eyes.
Continual wars and wives are what
Have tattered his ears and battered his head.

Like a bundle of old rope and iron
Sleeps till blue dusk. Then reappear
His eyes, green as ringstones : he yawns wide red,
Fangs fine as a lady's needle and bright.

A tomcat sprang at a mounted knight,
Locked round his neck like a trap of hooks
While the knight rode fighting its clawing and bite.
After hundreds of years the stain's there

On the stone where he fell, dead of the tom :
That was at Barnborough. The tomcat still
Grallochs odd dogs on the quiet,
Will take your head clean off your simple pullet,

Is unkillable. From the dog's fury,
From gunshot fired point-blank he brings
His skin whole, and whole
From owlish moons of bekittenings

Among ashcans. He leaps and lightly
Walks upon sleep, his mind on the moon.
Nightly over the round world of men,
Over the roofs go his eyes and outcry.

Ted Hughes

FOG

The fog comes
on little cat feet.

It sits looking
over harbour and city
on silent haunches
and then moves on

Carl Sandburg

THE FOG

Slowly, the fog,
Hunch-shouldered with a gray face,
Arms wide, advances,
Finger-tips touching the way
Past the dark houses
And dark gardens of roses.
Up the short street from the harbour,
Slowly the fog,
Seeking, seeking;
Arms wide, shoulders hunched,
Searching, searching.
Out through the streets to the fields,
Slowly the fog—
A blind man hunting the moon.

F. R. McCreary

THE SHIP

They have launched the little ship,
　　She is riding by the quay.
Like a young doe to the river,
　　She has trembled to the sea.

Her sails are shaken loose;
　　They flutter in the wind.
The cat's paws ripple round her
　　And the gulls scream behind.

The rope is cast, she moves
　　Daintily out and south,
Where the snarling ocean waits her
　　With tiger-foaming mouth.

Richard Church

WIND

This house has been far out at sea all night,
The woods crashing through darkness, the booming
hills,
Winds stampeding the fields under the window
Floundering black astride and blinding wet

Till day rose; then under an orange sky
The hills had new places, and wind wielded
Blade-light, luminous and emerald,
Flexing like the lens of a mad eye.

At noon I scaled along the house-side as far as
The coal-house door. I dared once to look up—
Through the brunt wind that dented the balls of my
eyes
The tent of the hills drummed and strained its
guyrope,

The fields quivering, the skyline a grimace,
At any second to bang and vanish with a flap:
The wind flung a magpie away and a black-
Back gull bent like an iron bar slowly. The house

Rang like some fine green goblet in the note
That any second would shatter it. Now deep
In chairs, in front of the great fire, we grip
Our hearts and cannot entertain book, thought,

Or each other. We watch the fire blazing,
And feel the roots of the house move, but sit on,
Seeing the window tremble to come in,
Hearing the stones cry out under the horizons.

Ted Hughes

HOUSE FOR SALE

The wind is loud, wraps noise about the house;
Night is a dark factory making sounds.
Outside the town, the last few trees plead,
Begging reprieve, but find they have no grounds.

Here, the walls are crumbling, windows tremble;
A new crack has spidered over the plaster;
The house should be disposed of before it falls down,
But who, in his right mind, would be its master?

Above this varicosed ceiling the children sleep;
Restlessly they mutter in the house's brain;
The eldest has a bag packed, ready, under the bed,
Will leave tomorrow on an early train.

Vernon Scannell

A WINDY DAY

The wind brings all dead things to life,
Branches that lash the air like whips
And dead leaves rolling in a hurry
Or peering in a rabbit's bury
Or trying to push down a tree;
Gates that fly open to the wind
And close again behind,
And fields that are a flowing sea
And make the cattle look like ships;
Straws glistening and stiff
Lying on air as on a shelf
And pond that leaps to leave itself;
And feathers too that rise and float,
Each feather changed into a bird,
And line-hung sheets that crack and strain;
Even the sun-greened coat,
That through so many winds has served,
The scarecrow struggles to put on again.

Andrew Young

THE HOUSE MARTINS

Pines I remember, the air crisp.
Here, in a haze, elms I see,
Do not see, and hills hiding the river.

But the roof is generous,
Can preserve nests. And again the martins mutter
Their small-talk, daily domestic twitter
After those miles, deadly to some,
Over glaciers, over high waves.

Arrived, arrived in whatever wind,
To ride all winds and, housed on the windy side,
Warm with their own blood the cold mud walls.

Michael Hamburger

RIDDLE

This wind wafts little creatures
High over the hill-slopes. They are very
Swarthy, clad in coats of black.
They travel here and there all together,
Singing loudly, liberal with their songs.
Their haunts are wooded cliffs, yet they sometimes
Come to the houses of men. Name them yourselves.

(*Answer p. 96*) *translated from the Old English
by Kevin Crossley-Holland*

THE POSTMAN

Satchel on hip
the postman goes
from doorstep to doorstep
and stooping sows

each letterbox
with seed. His right
hand all the morning makes
the same half circle. White

seed he scatters,
a fistful of
featureless letters
pregnant with ruin or love.

I watch him zig-
zag down the street
dipping his hand in that big
bag, sowing the cool, neat

envelopes which
make *twenty-one*
unaccountably rich,
twenty-two an orphan.

I cannot see
them but I know
others are watching. We
stoop in a row

(as he turns away),
straighten and stand
weighing and delaying
the future in one hand.

Jon Stallworthy

A REMOVAL FROM TERRY STREET

On a squeaking cart, they push the usual stuff,
A mattress, bed ends, cups, carpets, chairs,
Four paperback westerns. Two whistling youths
In surplus U.S. Army battle-jackets
Remove their sister's goods. Her husband
Follows, carrying on his shoulders the son
Whose mischief we are glad to see removed,
And pushing, of all things, a lawnmower.
There is no grass in Terry Street. The worms
Come up cracks in concrete yards in moonlight.
That man, I wish him well, I wish him grass.

Douglas Dunn

THRUSHES

The City Financier
walks in the gardens,
stiffly, because of
his pride and his burdens.

The daisies, looking
up, observe
only a self-
respecting curve.

The thrushes only
see a flat
table-land
of shiny hat.

He looks importantly
about him
while all the spring
gets on without him.

Humbert Wolfe

RIDDLE

In former days my mother and father
Forsook me for dead, for the fullness of life
Was not yet within me. But another woman
Graciously fitted me out in soft garments,
As kind to me as to her own children,
Tended and took me under her wing ;
Until under her shelter, unlike her kin,
I matured as a mighty bird (as was my fate).
My guardian then fed me until I could fly,
And could wander more widely on my
Excursions ; she had the less of her own
Sons and daughters by what she did thus.

(*Answer p. 96*) *translated from the Old English
by Kevin Crossley-Holland*

THAW ON A BUILDING SITE

The strong sun changed the air ; drops
Trembled down, expired upwards.
Saucer crusts of earth collapsed.
Extraordinary pools appeared.

And reddish planks turned yellow ;
A concrete mixer cleared its throat
For a boring speech, all consonants. Slow
Troglodytes came from the hut.

They swarmed in air, on earth, beneath it,
Crept in and out of space, informed
It with a ghost of shape—breathing
Not yet a language, but its grammar.

Wheelbarrows shot up thirty feet.
A ripped plank screamed. And, slowly, buildings
Backed their way into the light ;
They crumbled upwards into being.

Norman MacCaig

CRANES

Across a sky suddenly mid-February blue,
Over scaffolding that sketches where buildings are
coming up,
Clearly red cranes hand out portions of concrete,
Steel girders, rubble, clumsily like cold fingers
Getting used to themselves having been numb too
long.

J. R. S. Davies

THE BUILDERS

A cage flies up through scaffolding
Like a rocket through time.

Thirty-six floors,
The numbers in white on the windows.

High on the roof I see men clearly
In their yellow helmets, talking.

One of them laughs at something on the river.
A negro turns out his pockets.

Slowly a crane goes by,
Dragging a name through sky.

Hugo Williams

APRIL DAY: BINSEY

Now the year's let loose; it skips like a feckless
child,
Ruffles our hair, rouses the trees, runs wild,
Kisses the hills with sunlight, whips them with rain,
Tears the grass in passing, gets lost in the lane.
Taut as lyre-strings the swans' wings quiver,
Lyre-strings plucked by the wind on the swollen
river.
Shadow of cloud and cantering horses race
Over the meadows where heaven and earth embrace.

Michael Hamburger

APRIL RISE

If ever I saw blessing in the air
   I see it now in this still early day
Where lemon-green the vaporous morning drips
   Wet sunlight on the powder of my eye.

Blown bubble-film of blue, the sky wraps round
   Weeds of warm light whose every root and rod
Splutters with soapy green, and all the world
   Sweats with the bead of summer in its bud.

If ever I heard blessing it is there
   Where birds in trees that shoals and shadows are
Splash with their hidden wings and drops of sound
   Break on my ears their crests of throbbing air.

Pure in the haze the emerald sun dilates,
   The lips of sparrows milk the mossy stones,
While white as water by the lake a girl
   Swims her green hand among the gathered
   swans.

Now, as the almond burns its smoking wick,
   Dropping small flames to light the candled grass;
Now, as my low blood scales its second chance,
   If ever world were blessed, now it is.

Laurie Lee

GIRL, BOY, FLOWER, BICYCLE

This girl
Waits at the corner for
This boy
Freewheeling on his bicycle.
She holds
A flower in her hand
A gold flower
In her hand she holds
The sun.
With power between his thighs
The boy
Comes smiling to her
He rides
A bicycle that glitters like
The wind.
This boy this girl
They walk
In step with the wind
Arm in arm
They climb the level street
To where
Laid on the glittering handlebars
The flower
Is round and shining as
The sun.

M. K. Joseph

ON ROOFS OF TERRY STREET

Television aerials, Chinese characters
In the lower sky, wave gently in the smoke.

Next building sparrows peck at moss,
Urban flora and fauna, soft, unscrupulous.

Rain drying on the slates shines sometimes.
A builder is repairing someone's leaking roof,

He kneels upright to rest his back,
His trowel catches the light and becomes precious.

Douglas Dunn

A NEGRO WOMAN

carrying a bunch of marigolds
    wrapped
        in an old newspaper :
She carries them upright,
    bareheaded,
        the bulk
of her thighs
    causing her to waddle
        as she walks
looking into
    the store window which she passes
        on her way.

What is she
    but an ambassador
        from another world
a world of pretty marigolds
    of two shades
        which she announces

not knowing what she does
    other
        than walk the streets
holding the flowers upright
    as a torch
        so early in the morning.

William Carlos Williams

DAY OF THESE DAYS

Such a morning it is when love
leans through geranium windows
and calls with a cockerel's tongue.

When red-haired girls scamper like roses
over the rain-green grass,
and the sun drips honey.

when hedgerows grow venerable,
berries dry black as blood,
and holes suck in their bees.

Such a morning it is when mice
run whispering from the church,
dragging dropped ears of harvest.

When the partridge draws back his spring
and shoots like a buzzing arrow
over grained and mahogany fields.

When no table is bare,
and no breast is dry,
and the tramp feeds off ribs of rabbit.

Such a day it is when time
piles up the hills like pumpkins,
and the streams run golden.

When all men smell good,
and the cheeks of girls
are as baked bread to the mouth.

As bread and beanflowers
the touch of their lips,
and their white teeth sweeter than cucumbers.

Laurie Lee

SUMMER FARM

Straws like tame lightnings lie about the grass
And hang zigzag on hedges. Green as glass
The water in the horse-trough shines.
Nine ducks go wobbling by in two straight lines.

A hen stares at nothing with one eye,
Then picks it up. Out of an empty sky
A swallow falls and, flickering through
The barn, dives up again into the dizzy blue.

I lie, not thinking, in the cool, soft grass,
Afraid of where a thought might take me—as
This grasshopper with plated face
Unfolds his legs and finds himself in space.

Self under self, a pile of selves I stand
Threaded on time, and with metaphysic hand
Lift the farm like a lid and see
Farm within farm, and in the centre, me.

Norman MacCaig

PIGEONS

They paddle with staccato feet
In powder-pools of sunlight,
Small blue busybodies
Strutting like fat gentlemen
With hands clasped
Under their swallowtail coats ;
And, as they stump about,
Their heads like tiny hammers
Tap at imaginary nails
In non-existent walls.
Elusive ghosts of sunshine
Slither down the green gloss
Of their necks an instant, and are gone.

Summer hangs drugged from sky to earth
In limpid fathoms of silence :
Only warm dark dimples of sound
Slide like slow bubbles
From the contented throats.

Raise a casual hand—
With one quick gust
They fountain into air.

Richard Kell

APPLES

Behold the apples' rounded worlds :
juice-green of July rain,
the black polestar of flower, the rind
mapped with its crimson stain.

The russet, crab and cottage red
burn to the sun's hot brass,
they drop like sweat from every branch
and bubble in the grass.

They lie as wanton as they fall,
and where they fall and break,
the stallion clamps his crunching jaws,
the starling stabs his beak.

In each plump gourd the cidery bite
of boys' teeth tears the skin ;
the waltzing wasp consumes his share,
the bent worm enters in.

I, with an easy hunger, take
entire my season's dole ;
welcome the ripe, the sweet, the sour,
the hollow and the whole.

Laurie Lee

UNHARVESTED

A scent of ripeness from over a wall.
And come to leave the routine road
And look for what had made me stall,
There sure enough was an apple tree
That had eased itself of its summer load,
And of all but its trivial foliage free,
Now breathed as light as a lady's fan.
For there had been an apple fall
As complete as the apple had given man.
The ground was one circle of solid red.

May something go always unharvested !
May much stay out of our stated plan,
Apples or something forgotten and left,
So smelling their sweetness would be no theft.

Robert Frost

WINDFALLS

The windfalls ripen on the lawn,
The flies won't be disturbed.
They doze and glisten,
They wait for the fresh falls
To wipe them out.
          And now
Like warts, a pair of them sleep on your wrist.
Their wings are limp with apple juice ;
Disabled, sleek, they have their fill.

Another wind prepares. It will shake apples
For these suicidal flies. It will restore
To lethargy your pale, disfigured hand.

Ian Hamilton

BLACKBERRY-PICKING
For Philip Hobsbaum

Late August, given heavy rain and sun
For a full week, the blackberries would ripen.
At first, just one, a glossy purple clot
Among others, red, green, hard as a knot.
You ate that first one and its flesh was sweet
Like thickened wine : summer's blood was in it
Leaving stains upon the tongue and lust for
Picking. Then red ones inked up and that hunger
Sent us out with milk-cans, pea-tins, jam-pots
Where briars scratched and wet grass bleached our
boots.
Round hayfields, cornfields and potato-drills
We trekked and picked until the cans were full,
Until the tinkling bottom had been covered
With green ones, and on top big dark blobs burned
Like a plate of eyes. Our hands were peppered
With thorn pricks, our palms sticky as Bluebeard's.

We hoarded the fresh berries in the byre.
But when a bath was filled we found a fur,
A rat-grey fungus, glutting on our cache.
The juice was stinking too. Once off the bush
The fruit fermented, the sweet flesh would turn sour.
I always felt like crying. It wasn't fair
That all the lovely canfuls smelt of rot.
Each year I hoped they'd keep, knew they would not.

Seamus Heaney

EVENING AFTER RAIN

Nothing exactly says that it is evening.
The sun could be anywhere behind the cloud.
It is a matter of the daylight slowly altering,
The wet turquoise of grass and silverweed
Becoming slightly misty. Now the birds
Are tuning up ; some single notes begin.
A bubble of rain is in the thrush's words
And will not loosen, till he ends his song.

And nothing indicates that if an evening
This differs from the evenings one has known.
Only some expectation keeps one waiting,
Counting in the twilight of the lane
The petals, as they close. Until the sun's
Disc drops suddenly : under the cloud
A whitegold sky, the elms drip light, light runs,
Rinses and dazzles, down the rainwet road.

David Sutton

QUIET

The night was so quiet
That the hum of the candle burning
Came to my ear,
A sound of breath drawn through a reed
Far off.

The night was so quiet
That the air in the room
Poised, waiting to crack
Like a straining
Stick.

The night was so quiet
That the blood and flesh,
My visible self sunk in the chair,
Was a power-house giant, pulsing
Through the night.

Richard Church

HEDGEHOG

Twitching the leaves just where the drainpipe clogs
In ivy leaves and mud, a purposeful
Creature at night about its business. Dogs
Fear his stiff seriousness. He chews away

At beetles, worms, slugs, frogs. Can kill a hen
With one snap of his jaws, can taunt a snake
To death on muscled spines. Old countrymen
Tell tales of hedgehogs sucking a cow dry.

But this one, cramped by houses, fences, walls,
Must have slept here all winter in that heap
Of compost, or have inched by intervals
Through tiny gardens to this ivy bed.

And here, dim-eyed, but ears so sensitive
A voice within the house can make him freeze,
He scuffs the edge of danger; yet can live
Happily in our nights and absences.

A country creature, wary, quiet, and shrewd,
He takes the milk we give him, when we've gone.
At night, our slamming voices must seem crude
To one who sits and waits for silences.

Anthony Thwaite

THE LISTENERS

"Is anybody there?" said the Traveller,
Knocking on the moonlit door :
And his horse in the silence champed the grasses
Of the Forest's ferny floor ;
And a bird flew up out of the turret,
Above the Traveller's head ;
And he smote upon the door again a second time ;
"Is there anybody there?" he said.
But no one descended to the Traveller ;
No head from the leaf-fringed sill
Leaned over and looked into his grey eyes,
Where he stood perplexed and still.
But only a host of phantom listeners
That dwelt in the lone house then
Stood listening in the quiet of the moonlight
To the voice from the world of men ;
Stood thronging the faint moonbeams on the dark
stair,
That goes down to the empty hall,
Hearkening in an air stirred and shaken
By the lonely Traveller's call.
And he felt in his heart their strangeness,

Their stillness answering his cry,
While his horse moved, cropping the dark turf
'Neath the starred and leafy sky;
For he suddenly smote on the door, even
Louder, and lifted his head :—
''Tell them I came, and no one answered,
That I kept my word,'' he said.
Never the least stir made the listeners,
Though every word he spake

Fell echoing through the shadowiness of the
still house
From the one man left awake :
Ay, they heard his feet upon the stirrup,
And the sound of iron on stone,
And how the silence surged softly backward,
When the plunging hoofs were gone.

Walter de la Mare

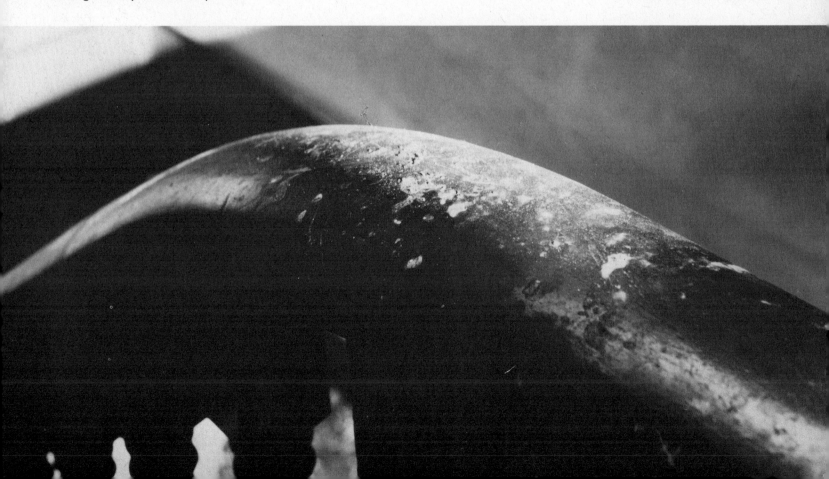

LATE NIGHT WALK DOWN TERRY STREET

A policeman on a low-powered motorcycle stops.
His radio crackles, his helmet yellows.

Empty buses heading for the depot
Rush past the open end of Terry Street.

In their light, a man with a bike walking home,
Too drunk to ride it, turns into Terry Street.

Taxis swerve down Terry Street's shortcut,
Down uneven halls of Street Lighting Department
Yellow,

Into which now comes the man with the bike,
Struggling to keep on his legs.

The policeman waits under a gone-out streetlamp.
He stops the drunk, they talk, they laugh together.

I pass them then, beside dark, quiet houses,
In others mumbling sounds of entertainment;

Cathode glows through curtains, faint latest tunes;
Creaking of bedsprings, lights going out.

Douglas Dunn

THE 'ALICE JEAN'

One moonlight night a ship drove in,
   A ghost ship from the west,
Drifting with bare mast and lone tiller;
   Like a mermaid drest
In long green weed and barnacles
   She beached and came to rest.

All the watchers of the coast
   Flocked to view the sight;
Men and women, streaming down
   Through the summer night,
Found her standing tall and ragged
   Beached in the moonlight.

Then one old woman stared aghast:
   'The *Alice Jean*? But no!
The ship that took my Ned from me
   Sixty years ago—
Drifted back from the utmost west
   With the ocean's flow?

'Caught and caged in the weedy pool
   Beyond the western brink,
Where crewless vessels lie and rot
   In waters black as ink,
Torn out at last by a sudden gale—
   Is it the *Jean*, you think?'

A hundred women gaped at her,
   The menfolk nudged and laughed,
But none could find a likelier story
   For the strange craft
With fear and death and desolation
   Rigged fore and aft.

The blind ship came forgotten home
   To all but one of these,
Of whom none dared to climb aboard her:
   And by and by the breeze

Veered hard about, and the *Alice Jean*
   Foundered in foaming seas.

Robert Graves

JOHN POLRUDDON

John Polruddon
All of a sudden
Went out of his house one night,

When a privateer
Came sailing near
Under his window-light.

They saw his jugs
His plates and mugs
His hearth as bright as brass,

His gews and gaws
And kicks and shaws
All through their spying-glass.

They saw his wine
His silver shine
They heard his fiddlers play.

Tonight, they said,
Out of his bed
Polruddon we'll take away.

And from a skiff
They climbed the cliff
And crossed the salt-wet lawn,

And as they crept
Polruddon slept
The night away to dawn.

In air or ground
What is that sound?
Polruddon said, and stirred.

They breathed, Be still,
It was the shrill
Of the scritch-owl you heard.

O yet again
I hear it plain,
But do I wake or dream?

In morning's fog
The otter-dog
Is whistling by the stream.

Now from the sea
What comes for me
Beneath my window dark?

Lie still, my dear,
All that you hear
Is the red fox's bark.

Swift from his bed
Polruddon was sped
Before the day was white,

And head and feet
Wrapped in a sheet
They bore him down the height.

And never more
Through his own door
Polruddon went nor came,

Though many a tide
Has turned beside
The cliff that bears his name.

On stone and brick
Was ivy thick,
And the grey roof was thin,

And winter's gale
With fists of hail
Broke all the windows in.

The chimney-crown
Is tumbled down
And up grew the green,

Till on the cliff
It was as if
A house had never been.

But when the moon
Swims late or soon
Across St. Austell Bay,

What sight, what sound
Haunts air and ground
Where once Polruddon lay?

It is the high
White scritch-owl's cry,
The fox as dark as blood,

And on the hill
The otter still
Whistles beside the flood.   *Charles Causley*

FROM THE NIGHT-WINDOW

The night rattles with nightmares.
Children cry in the close-packed houses,
A man rots in his snoring.
On quiet feet, policemen test doors.
Footsteps become people under streetlamps.
Drunks return from parties,
Sounding of empty bottles and old songs.
The young women come home,
The pleasure in them deafens me.
They trot like small horses
And disappear into white beds
At the edge of the night.
All windows open, this hot night,
And the sleepless, smoking in the dark,
Making small red lights at their mouths,
Count the years of their marriages.   *Douglas Dunn*

THE PROJECTIONIST'S NIGHTMARE

This is the projectionist's nightmare :
A bird finds its way into the cinema,
finds the beam, flies down it,
smashes into a screen depicting a garden,
a sunset and two people being nice to each other.
Real blood, real intestines, slither down
the likeness of a tree.
'This is no good,' screams the audience,
'This is not what we came to see.'

Brian Patten

INTERRUPTION TO A JOURNEY

The hare we had run over
Bounced about the road
On the springing curve
Of its spine.

Cornfields breathed in the darkness.
We were going through the darkness and
The breathing cornfields from one
Important place to another.

We broke the hare's neck
And made that place, for a moment,
The most important place there was,
Where a bowstring was cut

And a bow was broken for ever
That had shot itself through so many
Darknesses and cornfields.

It was left in that landscape.
It left us in another.

Norman MacCaig

AMBULANCE

they threw it
in a blanket
the colour of blood
and closed the doors

the windows
were black because
nobody wanted
to see the inside

we stood on
the pavement
as they hosed down
the street

and discussed
what it was

to be staying
alive

Miles Gibson

THE CASUALTY

Farmers in the fields, housewives behind steamed windows,
Watch the burning aircraft across the blue sky float,
As if a firefly and a spider fought,
Far above the trees, between the washing hung out.
They wait with interest for the evening news.

But already, in a brambled ditch, suddenly-smashed
Stems twitch. In the stubble a pheasant
Is craning every way in astonishment.
The hare that hops up, quizzical, hesitant,
Flattens ears and tears madly away and the wren warns.

Some, who saw fall, smoke beckons. They jostle above,
They peer down a sunbeam as if they expected there
A snake in the gloom of the brambles or a rare flower—
See the grave of dead leaves heave suddenly, hear
It was a man fell out of the air alive,

Hear now his groans and senses groping. They rip
The slum of weeds, leaves, barbed coils ; they raise
A body that as the breeze touches it glows,
Branding their hands on his bones. Now that he has
No spine, against heaped sheaves they prop him up,

Arrange his limbs in order, open his eye,
Then stand, helpless as ghosts. In a scene
Melting in the August noon, the burned man
Bulks closer greater flesh and blood than their own,
As suddenly the heart's beat shakes his body and the eye

Widens childishly. Sympathies
Fasten to the blood like flies. Here's no heart's more
Open or large than a fist clenched, and in there
Holding close complacency its most dear
Unscratchable diamond. The tears of their eyes

Too tender to let break, start to the edge
Of such horror close as mourners can,
Greedy to share all that is undergone,
Grimace, gasp, gesture of death. Till they look down
On the handkerchief at which his eye stares up.

Ted Hughes

SURVIVORS

With the ship burning in their eyes
The white faces float like refuse
In the darkness—the water screwing
Oily circles where the hot steel lies.

They clutch with fingers frozen into claws
The lifebelts thrown from a destroyer,
And see, between the future's doors,
The gasping entrance of the sea.

Taken on board as many as lived, who
Had a mind left for living and the ocean,
They open eyes running with surf,
Heavy with the grey ghosts of explosion.

The meaning is not yet clear,
Where daybreak died in the smile—
And the mouth remained stiff
And grinning, stupid for a little while.

But soon they joke, easy and warm
As men will who have died once
Yet somehow were able to find their way—
Muttering this was not included in their pay.

Later, sleepless at night, the brain spinning
With cracked images, they won't forget
The confusion and the oily dead,
Nor yet the casual knack of living.

Alan Ross

THE RESCUE

That's what we live on : thinking of their rescue
And fitting our future to it. You have to see it :

First, the dry smudge upon the sea-line,
Then the slow growth of a shipful of strangers
Into this existence. White bows, the white bow-wave
Cleaving the nightmare, slicing it open,
Letting in reality. Then all the sailors white
As maggots waving at the rail. Then their shouting—
Faintly at first, as you can think
The crowd coming with Christ sounded
To Lazarus in his cave.
Then the ship's horn giving blast after blast out
Announcing the end of the island. Then the rowboat.
I fancy I saw it happen. The five were standing
In the shallows with the deathly sea
Lipping their knees and the rattle of oar-locks
Shaking the sand out of their brain-cells,
The flash of wet oars slashing their eyes back alive—
All the time the long white liner anchoring the world
Just out there, crowded and watching.
Then there came a moment in the eternity of this island
When the rowboat's bows bit into the beach
And the lovely greetings and chatter scattered—
This is wrong.
                    The five never moved.
They just stood sucked empty
As grasses by this island's silence. And the crew
Helped them into the boat not speaking
Knowing the sound of a voice from the world
Might grab too cheery-clumsy
Into their powdery nerves. Then they rowed off
Toward the shining ship with carefully
Hushed oars dipping and squeaking. And the five sat all the time
Like mummies with their bandages lifted off—
While the ship's dazzling side brimmed up the sky
And leaned over, pouring faces.

Ted Hughes

PSALM OF THOSE WHO GO FORTH BEFORE DAYLIGHT

The policeman buys shoes slow and careful; the teamster buys gloves slow and careful; they take care of their feet and hands; they live on their feet and hands.

The milkman never argues; he works alone and no one speaks to him; the city is asleep when he is on the job; he puts a bottle on six hundred porches and calls it a day's work; he climbs two hundred wooden stairways; two horses are company for him; he never argues.

The rolling-mill men and the sheet-steel men are brothers of cinders; they empty cinders out of their shoes after their day's work; they ask their wives to fix burnt holes in the knees of their trousers; their necks and ears are covered with a smut; they scour their necks and ears; they are brothers of cinders.

Carl Sandburg

FATHER'S GLOVES

Not garments. A craftsman's armour
Worn to blunt the hooks of pain.
Massive, white asbestos mitts
He brought back from the shipyard
Hang cool by his blowlamp
And his sailmaker's palm.
In his hearth, treasured still,
Scored by remembered cinders,
Lie gauntlets from his dirt-track days
That sometimes, when his fire is dull,
He wears to prod the embers.

Keeping them rekindles him.

He keeps them all, the pairs
We give him on his birthdays,
Crammed in drawers too full to shut.
Some of them may have a use
At family ceremonial:
But, christening or funeral,
Pigskin, suede kid or calf,
We'd have him carry them, because
His hands are warmed with them off.

Ted Walker

SOIL

A field with tall hedges and a young
Moon in the branches and one star
Declining westward set the scene
Where he works slowly astride the rows
Of red mangolds and green swedes
Plying mechanically his cold blade.

This is his world, the hedge defines
The mind's limits ; only the sky

Is boundless, and he never looks up ;
His gaze is deep in the dark soil,
As are his feet. The soil is all ;
His hands fondle it, and his bones
Are formed out of it with the swedes.
And if sometimes the knife errs,
Burying itself in his shocked flesh,
Then out of the wound the blood seeps home
To the warm soil from which it came.

R. S. Thomas

KITE

when steel winds wiped
the forest to a smudge

and birds fell from
the startled hair
of trees

she knew
there was no time
allowed

to hide herself
beneath the grass

and as she bristled
with regret

the wind caught hold
her paper neck

and found the cord
just long enough

to hang her
in the morning air

Miles Gibson

GALE WARNING

The Wind breaks bound, tossing the oak and
chestnut,
Whirling the paper at street corners,
The city clerks are harassed, wrestling head-down:
The gulls are blown inland.

Three slates fall from a roof,
The promenade is in danger:
Inland, the summer fete is postponed,
The British glider record broken.

The wind blows through the City, cleansing,
Whipping the posters from the hoardings,
Tearing the bunting and the banner,
The wind blows steadily, and as it will.

Michael Roberts

THISTLES

Against the rubber tongues of cows and the hoeing
hands of men
Thistles spike the summer air
Or crackle open under a blue-black pressure.

Every one a revengeful burst
Of resurrection, a grasped fistful
Of splintered weapons and Icelandic frost thrust up

From the underground stain of a decayed Viking.
They are like pale hair and the gutturals of dialects.
Every one manages a plume of blood.

Then they grow grey, like men.
Mown down, it is a feud. Their sons appear,
Stiff with weapons, fighting back over the same
ground.

Ted Hughes

MUSHROOMS

Overnight, very
Whitely, discreetly,
Very quietly

Our toes, our noses
Take hold on the loam,
Acquire the air.

Nobody sees us,
Stops us, betrays us;
The small grains make room.

Soft fists insist on
Heaving the needles,
The leafy bedding,

Even the paving.
Our hammers, our rams,
Earless and eyeless,

Perfectly voiceless,
Widen the crannies,
Shoulder through holes. We

Diet on water,
On crumbs of shadow,
Bland-mannered, asking

Little or nothing.
So many of us!
So many of us!

We are shelves, we are
Tables, we are meek,
We are edible,

Nudgers and shovers
In spite of ourselves,
Our kind multiplies:

We shall by morning
Inherit the earth.
Our foot's in the door.

Sylvia Plath

DREAM

With a billhook
Whose head was hand-forged and heavy
I was hacking a stalk
Thick as a telegraph pole.
My sleeves were rolled
And the air fanned cool past my arms
As I swung and buried the blade,
Then laboured to work it unstuck.

The next stroke
Found a man's head under the hook.
Before I woke
I heard the steel stop
In the bone of the brow.

Seamus Heaney

THE HARVEST FIELD

There is nothing to note ; only the mowers
Moving like doom. Slowly, one by one,
A gloom of bees rises and soon snores
Thunder-headed away into the sun.

Listen ! Listen ! do you hear the hiss
Of the scythe in the long grasses
That are silently tingling like bells that kiss
And repel as the wind passes.

There in the last care and core of corn
The hare is couched : not till the mowers flash
Their smiling scythes, and all its walls are shorn
Will the wild creature dash
Into the wintry air of hound and horn.

Listen ! Listen ! do you hear the hiss
Of the scythe in the long grasses of your laughter ?
More is mowed than you know, for this
Is Time's swathe, and you are the one that he's
after.

W. R. Rodgers

MEN IN GREEN

Oh, there were fifteen men in green,
Each with a tommy-gun,
Who leapt into my plane at dawn ;
We rose to meet the sun.

We set our course towards the east
And climbed into the day
Till the ribbed jungle underneath
Like a giant fossil lay.

We climbed towards the distant range
Where two white paws of cloud
Clutched at the shoulders of the pass;
The green men laughed aloud.

They did not fear the ape-like cloud
That climbed the mountain crest
And hung from twisted ropes of air
With thunder in their breast.

They did not fear the summer's sun,
In whose hot centre lie
A hundred hissing cannon shells
For the unwatchful eye.

And when on Dobadura's field
We landed, each man raised
His thumb towards the open sky;
But to their right I gazed.

For fifteen men in jungle green
Rose from the kunai grass
And came towards the plane. My men
In silence watched them pass;
It seemed they looked upon themselves
In Time's prophetic glass.

Oh, there were some leaned on a stick
And some on stretchers lay
But few walked on their own two feet
In the early green of day.

They had not feared the ape-like cloud
That climbed the mountain crest;
They had not feared the summer's sun
With bullets for their breast.

Their eyes were bright, their looks were dull,
Their skin had turned to clay.
Nature had met them in the night
And stalked them in the day.

And I think still of men in green
On the Soputa track
With fifteen spitting tommy-guns
To keep a jungle back.

David Campbell

VIEW OF A PIG

The pig lay on a barrow dead.
It weighed, they said, as much as three men.
Its eyes closed, pink white eyelashes.
Its trotters stuck straight out.

Such weight and thick, pink bulk
Set in death seemed not just dead.
It was less than lifeless, further off.
It was like a sack of wheat.

I thumped it without feeling remorse.
One feels guilty insulting the dead,
Walking on graves. But this pig
Did not seem able to accuse.

It was too dead. Just so much
A poundage of lard and pork.
Its last dignity had entirely gone.
It was not a figure of fun.

Too dead now to pity.
To remember its life, din, stronghold
Of earthly pleasure as it had been,
Seemed a false effort, and off the point.

Too deadly factual. Its weight
Oppressed me—how could it be moved?
And the trouble of cutting it up!
The gash in its throat was shocking, but not pathetic.

Once I ran at a fair in the noise
To catch a greased piglet
That was faster and nimbler than a cat,
Its squeal was the rending of metal.

Pigs must have hot blood, they feel like ovens.
Their bite is worse than a horse's—
They chop a half-moon clean out.
They eat cinders, dead cats.

Distinctions and admirations such
As this one was long finished with.
I stared at it a long time. They were going to scald it,
Scald it and scour it like a doorstep.

Ted Hughes

THE LAST WHALE

the solitude of water
drove him mad

he wallowed like a zeppelin
full of holes

and when he landed
on the beach

they say he made
a thousand packs

of lightly salted
margarine

Miles Gibson

A DEAD MOLE

Strong-shouldered mole,
That so much lived below the ground,
Dug, fought and loved, hunted and fed,
For you to raise a mound
Was as for us to make a hole;
What wonder now that being dead
Your body lies here stout and square
Buried within the blue vault of the air?

Andrew Young

LITTLE FABLE

The mouse like halting clockwork, in the light
A shade of biscuit, curved towards the right

And hid behind the gas stove, peeping out
A sickly moment with its pencil snout.

Its run was blocked to keep it in the wall
But at the time it was not there at all.

The food is covered and a penny trap,
Being bought, is baited with a bacon scrap.

Its back is guillotined and seen to be
Grey and not brown, its feet formed properly.

Thus the obscene becomes pathetic and
What mind had feared is stroked by hand.

Roy Fuller

FIELD OF AUTUMN

Slow moves the acid breath of noon
Over the copper-coated hill,
slow from the wild crab's bearded breast
the palsied apples fall.

Like coloured smoke the day hangs fire,
taking the village without sound ;
the vulture-headed sun lies low
chained to the violet ground.

The horse upon the rocky height
rolls all the valley in his eye,
but dares not raise his foot or move
his shoulder from the fly.

The sheep, snail-backed against the wall,
lifts her blind face but does not know
the cry her blackened tongue gives forth
is the first bleat of snow.

Each bird and stone, each roof and well,
feels the gold foot of autumn pass ;
each spider binds with glittering snare
the splintered bones of grass.

Slow moves the hour that sucks our life,
slow drops the late wasp from the pear,
the rose tree's thread of scent draws thin—
and snaps upon the air.

Laurie Lee

GAME'S END

On autumn evenings the children still play in the
park,
Scuffing up the sweet-smelling aftermath,
Their shadows in the sunset triple length,
Making heroic kicks, half-legendary saves.
They play until it is dark,
And still for a little while after can be seen
By the flitting of their plimsolls, by their sleeves,
And by the twinkling orb of grass-stained polythene
Rising up white against dark sky or leaves.

Till, by some common consent, the game must close.
No one bothers any more to yell 'Pass' or 'Shoot',
Someone gives the ball a last terrific boot
Into the air and before it falls they are gone,
Wheeling away over the grass,
Snatching their sweaters up from the goalposts, going
Who knows where, only later to see how soon
The white ball never fell, but went on climbing
Into the dark air, and became the moon.

David Sutton

THROWING A TREE: NEW FOREST

The two executioners stalk along over the knolls,
Bearing two axes with heavy heads shining and wide,
And a long limp two-handled saw toothed for cutting great boles,
And so they approach the proud tree that bears the death-mark on its side.

Jackets doffed they swing axes and chop away just above ground,
And the chips fly about and lie white on the moss and fallen leaves;
Till a broad deep gash in the bark is hewn all the way round,
And one of them tries to hook upward a rope, which at last he achieves.

The saw then begins, till the top of the tall giant shivers:
The shivers are seen to grow greater each cut than before:
They edge out the saw, tug the rope; but the tree only quivers,
And kneeling and sawing again, they step back to try pulling once more.

Then, lastly, the living mast sways further sways: with a shout
Job and Ike rush aside. Reached the end of its long staying powers
The tree crashes downward: it shakes all its neighbours throughout
And two hundred years' steady growth has been ended in less than two hours.

Thomas Hardy

COAL FIRE

And once, in some swamp-forest, these,
My child, were trees.
Before the first fox thought to run,
These dead black chips were one
Green net to hold the sun.
Each leaf in turn was taught the right
Way to drink light:
The twigs were made to learn
How to catch flame and yet not burn;
Branch and then bough began to eat
Their diet of heat.
And so for years, six million years (or higher)
They held that fire.
And here, out of the splinters that remain,
The fire is loose again.
See how its little hands reach here and there,
Finger the air;
Then, growing bolder, twisting free,
It fastens on the remnant of the tree
And, one by one,
Consumes them, mounts beyond them, leaps, is done,
And goes back to the sun.

Louis Untermeyer

FOR BONFIRES

1

The leaves are gathered, the trees are dying for a time.
A seagull cries through white smoke in the garden fires
that fill the heavy air.
All day heavy air
is burning, a moody dog
sniffs and circles the swish of the rake.
In streaks of ash, the gardener drifting
ghostly, beats his hands, a cloud
of breath to the red sun.

2

An island in the city, happy demolition men
behind windowed hoardings—look at them
trailing drills through rubble dust, kicking rubble,
smoking leaning on a pick, putting the stub
over an ear and the hot yellow helmet over that,
whistling up the collapsing chimney, kicking the
ricochet, rattling the trail with
snakes of wire, slamming slabs
down, plaster, cornice, brick, brick
on broken brick and plaster dust,
sprawling with steaming cans and pieces
at noon, afternoon bare sweat shining
paths down chalky backs, coughing
in filtered sunshine, slithering, swearing,
joking, slowly stacking and building
their rubbish into a total bonfire.
Look at that Irishman, bending
in a beautiful arc to throw
the last black rafter to the top,
stands back, walks round it singing
as it crackles into flame—old doors,
old beams, boxes, window-frames,
a rag doll, sacks, flex, old newspapers,
burst shelves, a shoe, old dusters, rags of
wallpaper roses. And they all stand round,
and cheer the tenement to smoke.

3

In a galvanised bucket
the letters burn. They roar and twist
and the leaves curl back one by one.
They put out claws and scrape the iron
like a living thing,
but the scrabbling to be free soon subsides.
The black pages are fused
to a single whispering mass
threaded by dying tracks of gold.
Let them grow cold,
and when they're dead,
quickly draw breath.

Edwin Morgan

ROBIN

With a bonfire throat,
Legs of twig,
A dark brown coat,
The inspector robin
Comes where I dig.

Military man
With a bright eye
And a wooden leg,
He must scrounge and beg
Now the summer's by :

Beg at the doors,
Scrounge in the gardens,
While daylight lessens
And the grass glistens
And the ground hardens.

The toads have their vaults,
The squirrels their money,
The swifts their journey ;
For him the earth's anger,
The taste of hunger.

And his unfrightened song
For the impending snows
Is also for the rose
And for the great Armada
And the Phoenician trader
And the last missile raider—
It's the only one he knows.

Hal Summers

WINTER THE HUNTSMAN

Through his iron glades
Rides Winter the Huntsman.
All colour fades
As his horn is heard sighing.

For through the forest
His wild hooves crash and thunder
Till many a mighty branch
Is torn asunder.

And the red reynard creeps
To his hole near the river,
The copper leaves fall
And the bare trees shiver.

As night creeps from the ground,
Hides each tree from its brother,
And each dying sound
Reveals yet another.

Is it Winter the Huntsman
Who gallops through his iron glades,
Cracking his cruel whip
To the gathering shades ?

Osbert Sitwell

THE WINTER TREES

Against the evening sky the trees are black,
Iron themselves against the iron rails;
The hurrying crowds seek cinemas or homes,
A cosy hour where warmth will mock the wind.
They do not look at trees now summer's gone,
For fallen with the leaves are those glad days
Of sand and sea and ships, of swallows, lambs,
Of cricket teams, and walking long in woods.
Standing among the trees a shadow bends
And picks a cigarette-end from the ground;
It lifts the collar of an overcoat,
And blows upon its hands and stamps its feet—
For this is winter, chastiser of the free,
This is the winter, kind only to the bound.

Clifford Dyment

THE COMPUTER'S FIRST CHRISTMAS CARD

```
jollymerry
hollyberry
jollyberry
merryholly
happyjolly
jollyjelly
jellybelly
bellymerry
hollyheppy
jollyMolly
marryJerry
merryHarry
hoppyBarry
heppyJarry
boppyheppy
berryjorry
jorryjolly
moppyjelly
Mollymerry
Jerryjolly
bellyboppy
jorryhoppy
hollymoppy
Barrymerry
Jarryhappy
happyboppy
boppyjolly
jollymerry
merrymerry
merrymerry
merryChris
ammerryasa
Chrismerry
asMERRYCHR
YSANTHEMUM
```

Edwin Morgan

CHARTRES WINDOWS: WINTER

m y s t e r i o u s
  g l o o m
g l o o m
  l u m e
  l u m i n g
  l u m i n o u s
  i l l u m i n a t i n g
  i l l u m i n a t i o n
  g l o o m
  l o o m
  b l u e
  l u m i n o u s
m y s t e r i o u s
  b l u e
  b r e a t h
  i l l u m i n a t i n g
  r e d
  b l o o d
m y s t e r i o u s
 i n s p i r a t i o n

Paula Claire

SLEET

The first snow was sleet. It swished heavily
Out of a cloud black enough to hold snow.
It was fine in the wind, but couldn't bear to touch
Anything solid. It died a pauper's death.

Now snow — it grins like a maniac in the moon.
It puts a glove on your face. It stops gaps.
It catches your eye and your breath. It settles down
Ponderously crushing trees with its airy ounces.

But today it was sleet, dissolving spiders on
cheekbones,
Being melted spit on the glass, smudging the mind
That humped itself by the fire, turning away
From the ill wind, the sky filthily weeping.

Norman MacCaig

HOME

This weather won't let up. Above our heads
The houses lean upon each other's backs
And suffer the dark sleet that lashes them
Downhill. One window is alight.
'That's where I live'.

My father's sleepless eye
Is burning down on us. The ice
That catches in your hair melts on my tongue.

Ian Hamilton

SUNDAY AFTERNOONS

On Sunday afternoons
In winter, snow in the air,
People sit thick as birds
In the station buffet-bar.

They know one another.
Some exchange a few words
But mostly they sit and stare
At the urns and the rock buns.

Not many trains today.
Not many are waiting for trains
Or waiting for anything
Except for the time to pass.

The fug is thick on the glass
Beyond which, through honks and puffing,
An express shrugs and strains
To sidings not far away.

Here no one is saying good-bye:
Tears, promises to write,
Journeys, are not for them.
Here there are other things
To mull over, till the dark brings
Its usual burdensome
Thoughts of a place for the night,
A bit of warm and dry.

On Sunday afternoons
The loudspeaker has little to say
Of wherever the few trains go.
Not many are travellers.
But few are as still as these
Who sit here out of the snow,
Passing the time away
Till the night begins.

Anthony Thwaite

THE BATTLE

Helmet and rifle, pack and overcoat
Marched through a forest. Somewhere up ahead
Guns thudded. Like the circle of a throat
The night on every side was turning red.

They halted and they dug. They sank like moles
Into the clammy earth between the trees.
And soon the sentries, standing in their holes,
Felt the first snow. Their feet began to freeze.

At dawn the first shell landed with a crack.
Then shells and bullets swept the icy woods.
This lasted many days. The snow was black.
The corpses stiffened in their scarlet hoods.

Most clearly of that battle I remember
The tiredness in eyes, how hands looked thin
Around a cigarette, and the bright ember
Would pulse with all the life there was within.

Louis Simpson

OWLS

Two cinders of the fiery sunset
cooled in a tree-hole or stone-crevice sleep

awoke with moth-muffled wings to hook
the landscape in their flight.

In winter they flowed on white fields. The shrieking
silence
of the dark things in darkness was more magnetic
than light

a silence made luminous. One wingtwist made a
glow
of the white breast of one on the ridge as he watched
the other;

the wall was white from which they leapt
across field and canal to pin a mouse
and with no time for shock or shriek
a titbit was ferried to the one who watched at the
nest.

Once I roused one from his daytime half-sleep.
As he blundered drunken through the light

small birds skidded from him, gathered, and mobbed.
Strange dweller between day and night:

they say that someone dies
in the house over which he cries.

Glyn Hughes

THE THOUGHT-FOX

I imagine this midnight moment's forest:
Something else is alive
Beside the clock's loneliness
And this blank page where my fingers move.

Through the window I see no star:
Something more near
Though deeper within darkness
Is entering the loneliness:

Cold, delicately as the dark snow,
A fox's nose touches twig, leaf;
Two eyes serve a movement, that now
And again now, and now, and now

Sets neat prints into the snow
Between trees, and warily a lame
Shadow lags by stump and in hollow
Of a body that is bold to come

Across clearings, an eye,
A widening deepening greenness,
Brilliantly, concentratedly,
Coming about its own business

Till, with a sudden sharp hot stink of fox
It enters the dark hole of the head.
The window is starless still; the clock ticks,
The page is printed.

Ted Hughes

Acknowledgements

Our thanks are due to the following for permission to use copyright poems:

W. H. Auden for 'Their Lonely Betters'; Edward Brathwaite for 'The Cat'; Oxford University Press for Jon Stallworthy's 'First Blood' from *Out of Bounds* and Hugo Williams' 'The Builders' from *Sugar Daddy*; Angus & Robertson (UK) Ltd for David Campbell's 'The Man in Green' from *David Campbell Selected Poems 1942–1968*; Wm Heinemann Ltd for Richard Church's 'Quiet' and 'The Ship' from *Collected Poems*; The Poetry Society for Paula Claire's 'Chartres Windows: Winter'; Macmillan & Co. Ltd for George Macbeth's 'Bats' and 'The Wasps' Nest', Kevin Crossley Holland's 'Three Anglo-Saxon Riddles' from *The Battle of Maldon and Other Poems,* Charles Causley's 'John Polruddon', Thomas Hardy's 'Throwing a Tree: New Forest' and Glynn Hughes' 'Owl' from *Neighbours; New Statesman* for J. R. S. Davies' 'Cranes'; Jonathan Cape Ltd for C. Day-Lewis' 'The Fox' from *The Room and Other Poems*, Robert Frost's 'The Runaway' and 'Unharvested' from *The Poetry of Robert Frost* and Ted Walker's 'Polecats in Breconshire' and 'Father's Gloves' from *The Solitaires*; the Literary Trustees of Walter de la Mare and The Society of Authors for Walter de la Mare's 'The Listeners'; J. M. Dent & Sons for Clifford Dyment's 'The Winter Trees' from *Collected Poems*; Andre Deutsch for Roy Fuller's 'Little Fable' from *Collected Poems*; Methuen & Co. for Miles Gibson's 'Ambulance', 'Hedgehog', 'Kite' and 'The Last Whale' from *The Guilty Bystander*;

Faber & Faber Ltd for Douglas Dunn's 'Late Night Walk down Terry Street', 'From the Night Window', 'A Removal from Terry Street' and 'On Roofs of Terry Street' from *Terry Street*, Thom Gunn's 'Considering the Snail' from *My Sad Captains*, Ian Hamilton's 'Windfalls' and 'Home' from *The Visit*, Seamus Heaney's 'Trout' and 'Blackberry Picking' from *Death of a Naturalist*, 'Dream' from *Door Into the Dark* and Ted Hughes' 'The Horses', 'Wind', 'The Casualty' and 'The Thought Fox' from *The Hawk in the Rain*, 'Esther's Tomcat', 'View of a Pig' from *Lupercal*, 'Thistles' and 'The Rescue' from *Wodwo*, and Michael Roberts' 'Gale Warning' from *Collected Poems*, Robert Graves for 'The Alice Jean' from *The Penny Fiddle*; Michael Hamburger for 'Cat' and 'House Martins' from *Travelling* and 'April Day: Binsey' from *Poems 1950–1951*; M. K. Joseph and *Landfall* for 'Boy, Flower, Bicycle and Girl'; James Kirkup for 'The Caged Bird in Springtime'; Chatto & Windus for Richard Kell's 'Pigeons' from *Differences* and Jon Stallworthy's 'The Postman' from *Root and Branch*; Wm Heinemann Ltd, Laurence Pollinger Ltd and the Estate of the late Mrs Frieda Lawrence for D. H. Lawrence's 'Mountain Lion' and 'Two Performing Elephants' from *Complete Poems of D. H. Lawrence*; Laurie Lee for 'Day of these Days' 'April Rise' and 'Field of Autumn' and Andre Deutsch for 'Apples'; Edinburgh University Press for Edwin Morgan's 'Bonfires' from *Scottish Poetry Three* and 'The Computer's First Christmas Card' from *The Second Life*; F. R. McReary for 'The Fog'; The Hogarth Press for Norman MacCaig's 'Interruption to a Journey' from *Surroundings*, 'Feeding Ducks' from *A Common Grace*, 'Thaw on a Building Site' from *A Round of Applause*, 'Sleet' from *Measures* and 'Summer Farm' from *Riding Lights*; Allen & Unwin Ltd for Brian Patten's 'You'd Better Believe Him', 'A Small Dragon' and 'The Projectionist's Nightmare' from *Notes to the Hurrying Man*; Faber & Faber Ltd © Ted Hughes (London) 1967 and Alfred Knopf Inc., N.Y. © Sylvia Plath 1962 for 'Mushrooms' from *The Colossus*; Martin Secker & Warburg Ltd for W. R. Rodgers' 'The Harvest Field' from *Europa and the Bull*; University of London Press for T. W. Ramsey's 'Caught by Chance' from *Endymion to Silver*; Holt, Rinehart and Winston Inc., N.Y. © 1916, © 1944 by Carl Sandburg and Jonathan Cape for Carl Sandburg's 'Fog' from *Chicago Poems*; Eyre and Spottiswoode Ltd. for Alan Ross's 'Survivors'; G. T. Sassoon and the Estate of the late Siegfried Sassoon for 'Together' from *Collected Poems*; Vernon Scannell for 'House for Sale'; Barrie & Jenkins Ltd for E. J. Scovell's 'Boy Fishing' from *Shadows of Chrysanthemums*; Charles Scribner's Sons for 'The Battle' from *Good News of Death and Other Poems* © Louis Simpson (*Poets of Today* II); Chatto & Windus for Jon Silkin's 'Caring for Animals' from *The Peaceable Kingdom*; Gerald Duckworth & Co. for Osbert Sitwell's 'Winter the Huntsman' from *Selected Poems Old and New*; Hal Summers for 'Robin'; Rapp & Whiting Ltd for David Sutton's 'Starlings', 'Evening after Rain' and 'Game's End'; Oxford University Press for Anthony Thwaite's 'Hedgehog' and 'Sunday Afternoons' from *The Owl in the Tree*; Gaberbocchus Press for Stefan Themerson's 'shape' poem; Rupert Hart-Davis Ltd for R. S. Thomas' 'Soil' from *Song at the Year's Turning* and Andrew Young's 'Hard Frost', 'A Windy Day, 'A Dead Mole' from *The Collected Poems of Andrew Young*; Mrs Myfanwy Thomas for Edward Thomas' 'The Gallows'; Harcourt Brace Jovanovich for Louis Untermeyer's 'Coal Fire' from *Long Feud* © 1928, renewed 1956 by Louis Untermeyer; Miss Ann Wolfe for Humbert Wolfe's 'Thrushes' from *Kensington Gardens* (Benn); The Bodley Head for Rex Warner's 'Mallard' from *Poems and Contradictions* and MacGibbon & Kee Ltd for William Carlos Williams' 'Negro Woman' from *Pictures from Breughel*.

We would also like to thank the following for permission to reprint copyright photographs and other material (page numbers in brackets):

Aerofilms (37); J. Allan Cash (32, 67, 73); Mike Andrews (81, 85); Peter Baker (1, 69, 70); Barnaby's Picture Library (13, 14, 16, 20, 21, 25, 26 right, 33, 41, 43, 46, 48, 56–57, 80); Camera Press (18–19, 29, 40, 60–61, 90); Bruce Coleman (35); Bob Collins (53, 54, 77, 82); James Davis (34); Richard Gee (2–3, 6, 9, 17); Noelene Kelly (51, 66, 78); Keystone Press Agency (47, 62, 64); Musee National Fernand Leger (87); Monitor press Features (44); Louis & Daphne Peek (11, 74), Picturepoint (89); Paul Popper (26 left, 36, 75, 82, 86) John Sanders (24, 49); Spectrum (2–3, 6, 22–23, 45, 65, 76).

INDEX

AUDEN, W. H.
Their Lonely Betters 27
BRATHWAITE, EDWARD
The Cat 32
CAMPBELL, DAVID
Men in Green 70
CAUSLEY, CHARLES
John Polruddon 57
CHURCH, RICHARD
The Ship 35
Quiet 52
CLAIRE, PAULA
Chartres Windows : Winter 87
CROSSLEY-HOLLAND, KEVIN
Riddle 23
Riddle 38
Riddle 39
DAVIES, J. R. S.
Cranes 41
DE LA MARE, WALTER
The Listeners 52
DUNN, DOUGLAS
A Removal from Terry Street 39
On Roofs of Terry Street 44
Late Night Walk Down Terry Street 55
From the Night-Window 58
DYMENT, CLIFFORD
The Winter Trees 85
FROST, ROBERT
The Runaway 28
Unharvested 50
FULLER, ROY
Little Fable 72
GIBSON, MILES
Hedgehog 22
Ambulance 60
Kite 66
The Last Whale 72
GRAVES, ROBERT
The 'Alice Jean' 56
GUNN, THOMAS
Considering the Snail 23

HAMBURGER, MICHAEL
Cat 32
The House Martins 38
April Day : Binsey 42
HAMILTON, IAN
Windfalls 50
Home 88
HARDY, THOMAS
Throwing a Tree : New Forest 75
HEANEY, SEAMUS
Dawn Shoot 12
Trout 17
Blackberry-Picking 51
Dream 69
HUGHES, GLYN
Owls 91
HUGHES, TED
The Horses 15
Pike 18
Esther's Tomcat 33
Wind 36
The Casualty 60
The Rescue 62
Thistles 68
View of a Pig 71
The Thought-Fox 91
JOSEPH, M. K.
Girl, Boy, Flower, Bicycle 42
KELL, RICHARD
Pigeons 47
KIRKUP, JAMES
The Caged Bird in Springtime 30
LAWRENCE, D. H.
Mountain Lion 10
Two Performing Elephants 27
LEE, LAURIE
April Rise 42
Day of These Days 45
Apples 50
Field of Autumn 73
LEWIS, C. DAY
The Fox 27

MACBETH, GEORGE
  The Wasps' Nest 15
  Bats 26
MacCAIG, NORMAN
  Feeding Ducks 12
  Thaw on a Building Site 40
  Summer Farm 46
  Interruption to a Journey 60
  Sleet 88
McCREARY, F. R.
  The Fog 34
MORGAN, EDWIN
  For Bonfires 79
  The Computer's First Christmas Card 86
PATTEN, BRIAN
  You'd Better Believe Him 9
  A Small Dragon 28
  The Projectionist's Nightmare 59
PLATH, SYLVIA
  Mushrooms 68
RAMSEY, T. W.
  Caught by Chance 29
ROBERTS, MICHAEL
  Gale Warning 66
RODGERS, W. R.
  The Harvest Field 70
ROSS, ALAN
  Survivors 62
SANDBURG, CARL
  Fog 34
  Psalm of Those Who Go Forth Before Daylight 64
SASSOON, SIEGFRIED
  Together 28
SCANNELL, VERNON
  House for Sale 37
SCOVELL, E. J.
  The Boy Fishing 11
SILKIN, JON
  Caring for Animals 30
SIMPSON, LOUIS
  The Battle 90
SITWELL, OSBERT
  Winter the Huntsman 84

STALLWORTHY, JON
  First Blood 13
  The Postman 38
SUMMERS, HAL
  Robin 83
SUTTON, DAVID
  Starlings 15
  Evening After Rain 51
  Game's End 74
THEMERSON, STEFAN
  'Shape Poem' 31
THOMAS, EDWARD
  The Gallows 14
THOMAS, R. S.
  Soil 65
THWAITE, ANTHONY
  Hedgehog 52
  Sunday Afternoons 88
UNTERMEYER, LOUIS
  Coal Fire 79
WALKER, TED
  Polecats in Breconshire 22
  Father's Gloves 64
WARNER, REX
  Mallard 24
WHITMAN, WALT
  The Beasts 17
WILLIAMS, ERIC
  Stonehenge Sunset 2
WILLIAMS, HUGO
  The Builders 41
WILLIAMS, WILLIAM CARLOS
  A Negro Woman 44
WOLFE, HUMBERT
  Thrushes 39
YOUNG, ANDREW
  Hard Frost 11
  A Windy Day 37
  A Dead Mole 72

Answers to Riddles
Page 23 Swan
Page 38 Swallow
Page 39 Cuckoo